W9-BAL-125

BUDDHA
BEADS

Serenity In The Palm Of Your Hand
BUDDHA BEADS
Joanna Arettam
METRO BOOKS
NEW YORK

Book originally published as *Dharma Beads*



This 2009 edition published by Metro Books,
by arrangement with Tuttle Publishing.



Package design by Jo Obarowski
Book design by Carole Goodman/Blue Anchor Design

This book is part of the *Buddha Beads* kit and is not to be sold separately.

Metro Books
122 Fifth Avenue
New York, NY 10011

ISBN: 978-1-4351-0909-4

Printed and bound in China

1 3 5 7 9 10 8 6 4 2

# Acknowledgments

Among the many people who contributed information to this project, several stand out for their generosity and kindness. Guru Kirn Kaur Kalsa, a disciple of Yogi Bhajan, is a teacher of Kundalini yoga, the author of *Mala Meditation*, and a mala maker; she shared her insights on chanting and meditating with the mala. Through their company Shakya Design, Kate and David Cowsky, who are lay ministers in the order of Buddhist Contemplatives at Shasta Abbey in Mt. Shasta, California, create the malas that are sold there; they shared information on mala making. *The History of Beads* author Lois Sherr Dubin shared freely her knowledge of prayer beads, as did bead collector Phila McDaniel, who spoke from her travel experience in Tibet. Thank you.

A monk from Lijiang, China dressed in elaborate robes indicating his elevated position, with the simple mala beads he always carries and uses for meditation. The prayer wheel in his left hand contains papers with prayers written on them, which are released into the spiritual realm when the wheel is spun.

# *Contents*

# Introduction

*Buddha Beads* contains all the materials and instructions you need to make three beautiful 27-bead wrist malas: one each of fragrant sandalwood, earthy red carnelian, and glistening tiger's eye. Whether you use malas to relax, meditate, affirm your personal power, or to attract luck, prosperity, or well-being, we'll help you make them a part of your life.



Buddha bracelet. Yogic rosary. Mala beads. All describe the prayer-bead strands that have been used in meditation by Buddhists and Hindus for centuries. Usually they come in 27-, 54-, or 108-bead lengths. As so-called *power beads*, usually around 20 beads and so not exactly traditional, they have crossed over into popular culture—part fad, part good-luck charm. These bracelets grace the wrists of celebrities as well as hip students and smart young professionals around the country. But power beads are more than just a fashion statement. Used meditatively, they offer a scenic rest stop on the eight-lane highway of life—the scenery being that inner landscape of self-reflection.

In Hindu tradition, *Dharma* means duty to your class and stage of life. In Buddhism, it means accepting the truth of *karma* and reincarnation as taught by Buddha. But a more secular meaning of Dharma is simply to conduct your life in an ethical way. Just be a good person.

See? Mom was right.

Above right, Richard Gere, one of the most famous of American Buddhists, is frequently pictured with his mala beads.

Left, Monks gathered for prayer at the Jokhang. Because it is considered to be the most revered religious structure in Tibet, the ceremonies held here hold special significance.

Buddha
Beads:
Serenity
in the
Palm
of Your
Hand

Arahant Khema, the beautiful queen who was drawn to the love and wisdom of Buddha and became one of the two female disciples in charge of the order of nuns. Buddhist nuns traditionally shave their heads as a renunciation of worldly beauty. In her right hand she holds a mala of rosebuds.

Like the bodhi tree that springs from the earth to branch out in many directions, Buddhism in all its offshoots grows out of the sacred ground of Hinduism. Malas are shared by both religions. The word *mala* is Sanskrit for *garland of flowers*, and, as the word suggests, a long mala may be worn around the neck in the same way you would wear such a garland. But with a religious mala, each "flower" is a bead; each bead, a mantra or prayer. When you pray with a mala, you bring mind, heart, and body into the stillness of contemplation.

In Buddhist meditation, you reflect on the Dharma, the teachings of a supremely gifted yet mortal man who attained a state of enlightenment—*nirvana*. By accepting his truth—that there is a way out of the endless cycle of birth and death—and by following his path of kindness, compassion, and right living, you will find for yourself that place of eternal bliss.



Yet you need not be a Buddhist to bring malas into your life. Whatever your spiritual practice, you can engage a mala to help you create and maintain a state of quiet reflection—a cloister of the mind—where stress, negative emotions, and the noise of the world remain locked outside its gates. Let's look at the three types of malas you can use and some of the ways you can use them.

## Three different lengths

Malas come in three lengths, with the total number of beads in each having nine as their common denominator. You'll notice all have one large bead, which marks both the beginning and end of a prayer cycle, and many have beads of a contrasting color or material at specific intervals. The interval beads, not included in the count, are places for a reflective pause. The longer strands may be closed with an additional three beads, which represent the Buddhist concept of the Three Precious Jewels: Buddha, his teachings (the Dharma), and the larger community of believers (the Sangha).

There is also a place for ornamentation if it is symbolic of Buddhist themes. One beautiful finial is a finely wrought arabesque of threads reminiscent of the Endless Knot, an emblem not only of infinity but of the boundless wisdom and patience of the Buddha. Another is a simple tassel of the sort you might find on a lampshade or curtain pull. Attached to the mala, it takes on deeper significance, say the contemplatives at Shasta Abbey: "The tassel represents the roots of the lotus from which grow the stem and flower of enlightenment."

## 108 beads

In Hindu tradition, 108 is sacred. It is the number that results from multiplying the twelve astrological signs by the nine planets (the entire known universe when this formula was conceived millennia ago). Beads of this length are traditionally used in monastic practice. Devotees may wear them around the neck or coiled around the wrist when they are not engaged in prayer. "When you meditate an affirmation 108 times, you master that affirmation," says Guru Kirn.

On her way to the sacred temple in Lhasa, Tibet, this pilgrim carries a 108-bead mala with beads of contrasting color to mark prayer cycles. She also carries a prayer wheel.

## 54 beads

The malas you take out into the world are the "short form," easy to carry in a pouch or pocket and easy to use. The 54-length strand is exactly half the length of the traditional mala. If you are counting prayers, you would circle this mala twice. Even if specific prayer cycles are not your prime concern, you may find the length both comforting and convenient.

## 27 beads

This is the length you will make. Your mala is exactly the same as one a practicing Buddhist would wear. American Buddhists who live and work in the world rather than in a monastic environment often prefer the wrist-style rosary—worn, by the way, on the left wrist—because although it is a meditative touchstone, its jewelry-like appearance allows it to blend in with more secular ornamentation. You can appreciate the irony of wrist malas *becoming* secular ornamentation—love beads for the new millennium.

## Using the mala in meditation or prayer

Most of us who live in the Western Hemisphere understand the concept of prayer. Often it's an entreaty, in words learned by rote in childhood, directed to a particular spiritual entity as you sit or kneel. Meditation may seem more mysterious, more exotic. Do you sit in lotus position? Do you burn incense? Do you chant? You can do all of the above—but you don't have to. Both prayer and meditation focus your mind and center your spirit. As you travel bead by bead around the mala, you may use whatever medium works for you—a Western prayer, an Eastern mantra, or an affirmation from your own heart.

You may direct your prayer/meditation to a holy exemplar such as Jesus, the Virgin Mary, Allah, the Buddha, or Kuan Yin, who is beloved among all the bodhisattvas. (A *bodhisattva* is an enlightened being so compassionate that she or he has delayed entry into nirvana to help all others along the path to enlightenment.) Alternatively, you may direct your love or prayerful energy toward someone who would benefit emotionally or physically from your spiritual gift.



"Prayer works," says Guru Kirn, expressing a thought that is familiar to even the most undisciplined worshipper. Putting the concept in broader terms, she adds, "Meditating with a mala crosses all boundaries of culture and religion." Here are some suggestions from various sources to help you focus and channel spiritual energy with your mala.

Buddhist nuns beg for alms. Begging is looked upon as a service because it allows donors to raise their merit and thereby affect their own reincarnation.

Malas help focus our attention during meditation. They are also used to count repetitions of mantras or sutras.

## A secular mantra

This simple mantra, **Light, Love, Peace**, comes from Guru Kirn. You'll go around your mala, bead by bead. On the first bead after the guru bead, say *Light*. On the second, say *Love*. On the third, say *Peace*. Continue around the rosary, reflecting on the ideas behind those words. When you get to the guru bead, point it outward and say, *Light before me, light behind me, light above me, light below me, light to the left of me, light to the right of me, light to my environment.* Then repeat the mantra using *Love* and then *Peace*.

"If you've had a negative experience with a person, envision that person and do the mantra," says Guru Kirn. The same goes for a difficult experience or situation.

Known as Hotei in Japan (where this figure is from) and Putai in China, he is always shown with a beggar's sack on his back and frequently with a mala in his hand. He is also known as the Laughing Buddha.

## Two yogic mantras

The first mantra is called **Har**. Just *Har* over and over, bead by bead, breath by breath. But don't be fooled by its simplicity. "*Har* is a name of God that invokes abundance, prosperity, and energy. It's a key that opens the heart," says Guru Kirn. "To pronounce *Har* correctly, there are two things you need to know," she says. "First, the short 'a' in *Har* is like the 'u' in 'hut.' Second, when you pronounce the 'r', strike the upper palate of the mouth with the tip of your tongue. This will stimulate the proper meridian points."

The second mantra, for purification and rejuvenation, is called **Sat Nam**, which you'll chant bead by bead. *Sat* is truth; *Nam* is identity. "It will eliminate negative thought patterns," says Guru Kirn. To chant it correctly, *Sat* is pronounced like "hut"; *Nam* is like "calm." Let the tongue strike the upper palate of the mouth just behind the two front teeth on *Sat*, pulling in the navel quickly as you say it. *Nam* is light, like a breath out. "Reciting this mantra will change the secretions of your hypothalamus to enhance your higher virtues," says Guru Kirn.

For more specific information on pronunciation and breathing as you do these mantras, and for additional mantras, refer to Guru Kirn's book *Mala Meditation* (see Resources, pg. 79).

### Three Buddhist mantras

If you are new to the concepts of Buddhist philosophy, you might recite aloud (or quietly to yourself) this first mantra, the **Three Precious Jewels of Buddhism**. At each bead, say: *Homage to the Buddha, Homage to the Dharma, Homage to the Sangha* as you reflect on the life of Buddha, his teachings, and your involvement in a community of believers. Sangha is a group of seekers who gather around a master in order to attain spiritual knowledge and realization of the highest truth.

Kuan Yin, Goddess of Mercy, is the popular bodhisattva of compassion and kindness. Calling on Kuan Yin can provide relief from fear, danger, and depression.

White Tara Bodhisattva statue in Asakusa Park, Tokyo, Japan, which surrounds Sensou Temple, the oldest Buddhist shrine in Japan. Tara is especially venerated among Tibetan Buddhists.

A beautiful mantra in Sanskrit is *Om Mane Padme Hum*, which means "Hail, Jewel in the Lotus." The "Jewel" is Kuan Yin, Bodhisattva of Compassion. The "Lotus" is the thousand-petaled blossom of enlightenment. *Mane* is pronounced as two syllables evenly stressed: ma nay. So is *padme*: pahd may. Recite the entire mantra in one breath, letting each syllable resonate within your chest and throat. Repeat the mantra as you move around the mala bead by bead. If you would prefer to chant in English, you might say: *Hail, Kuan Yin, Bodhisattva of Compassion*. Kuan Yin is known as Kannon in Japan and Avalokiteshvara in India.

A third mantra calls upon Tara. For Tibetan Buddhists, she is the Bodhisattva of Compassion. Exceptionally lovely, Tara is always portrayed seated on a moon disc supported by a giant lotus flower. White Tara sits cross-legged in lotus position. Green Tara extends one leg, as if to reach out to a supplicant. In either form, Tara guides all seekers beyond fear into eternity. It is said that merely by uttering her name, *Tara*, she will respond. If you wish a longer mantra, say *Om Tare Tam Svaha* in one deeply resonant breath. In this mantra, Tam is the sound that contains Tara's essence. Tare is pronounced "ta ray." Svaha is pronounced as it looks: sva ha. All the a's are sounded as "ah."

## Personal affirmations

With a personal affirmation you channel your consciousness into a positive state so that you can make changes within yourself for the better. Think of a personal affirmation as your psychic best friend, the one who pulls you away from an unhealthy situation, applauds you when you've done well, and simply shares in your good fortune. You can create personal affirmations for all the situations in your life. Simply tapping your creative energy to create the mantra begins the process by which you can realize its outcome. A handful of suggestions:



TO RELEASE TENSION: *I will no longer be tied up by the bonds of stress. Bead by bead, I loosen the binding around me. My chest expands more fully. My heart opens. My muscles relax into themselves. I remain responsible, but my responsibilities do not restrain me.*

TO STOP SMOKING: *I breathe. I breathe. I breathe. With each breath in, I feel the energy of life as oxygen fills my lungs, my bloodstream, and my being. With each breath out, I feel the energy of purity as the toxins that I have carried within me dissipate into thin air.*

TO ACCESS CREATIVE ENERGY *I can create with my hands, head, and heart. I add bead after bead to my mala and remind myself that all creative work is done one step at a time.*



TO BUILD SELF-ESTEEM *I am worthy and worthwhile. I breathe in the positive feelings about myself and feel them expand into all of my corners. I exhale the negative feelings about myself and watch them disappear as they leave my body.*

## What is a mantra?

A mantra is a sound or word you utter, usually repeatedly, to focus your consciousness. Om, for instance, is the primal sound—the vibration of the universe. Intoning the sound aligns your own vibration with that of the infinite, beginning a transformation within you that helps raise you to a higher, clearer state of consciousness. The most powerful mantras stimulate meridians in the mouth and head, which helps open the Eye and Crown chakras.

A gilded wall painting in the ruins of Ronbuk Monastery beneath Chomolugma (Mt. Everest) at 29,108 feet.

A
Drop of
Infinity

Splendidly, impossibly round with a surface that falls onto itself over and over and over again, a sphere is the shape of totality. From Gaia, our luminous planet, outward to the resplendent orbs that surround us, the unimaginable vastness of the celestial universe is filled with whirling spheres of gas and matter. We now know that a similar vastness stretches invisibly at the subatomic level, where almost immeasurably minuscule spheres orbit in the space contained by objects we perceive as solid.

A perfectly round bead lies somewhere between those two realms. Poised between two fingertips or cradled in the palm of the hand, it conjures infinity in a way our finite minds can understand. Strung into a circle to be worn or prayed with, it is infinity made intimate.

Although the earliest humans understood cyclical time—the sun, after all, rose and set each day—it's unlikely they could have conceived of infinity. But they were moved by the power of a simple round bead. By the New Stone Age, some 30,000 years ago, they were chipping stone, bone, and amber into beads and stringing them into objects of personal and talismanic adornment.



Mala beads are more than adornment. Although they may be worn at the wrist or around the neck, they provide a means of counting prayers for Hindu and Buddhist devotees. The earliest known mala rosary is about 2,000 years old. Its existence is nothing short of miraculous, for it was strung from seeds, a hardly durable material (as Hindu malas still are). But malas surely existed back farther in time because Hinduism, even two millennia ago, was an ancient religion. More than 1,500 years before the birth of Christ, it had taken root in the hearts, minds, and soil of India.

Holding a Rudrasksha seed mala, this Tibetan Yogi also holds a skull cup containing milk for an offering. The skull represents the severing of human desires, which is necessary to reach enlightenment and nirvana. Often the skulls are those of a revered, deceased teacher.

So how does a rosary from a 2,500-year-old religion become trendy in contemporary American culture?

"Consider its basic design," says fashion editor Elissa D'Elia, commenting on the wrist mala. "It rolls, it stretches, it feels good on the wrist. It's unisex, so everyone can wear it." Moreover, says D'Elia, who took the on-the-street photos you see on the left, "The mala evokes a sense of inner knowing. Being able to select your own colors makes wearing it a very personal experience. And the deeper meaning, the power, of the various stones brings something spiritual to our lives."

Outside the Potala Palace in Tibet (right), women sell Buddhist ritual objects, including skull cups, bells, dorjes, tinkshas, thigh bone trumpets, purbas, prayer wheels, knives, jewelry, and Gau boxes that hold Buddhist prayers. Many of these items are sold to tourists who come to see this former Winter Palace of the Dalai Lama. On the streets of New York (left), you can buy various length malas and power beads, among other ethnic, ritual objects.

How authentic are the malas sold on the street? That varies from vendor to vendor, depending on the source. Look for 27 beads (not counting the larger guru bead). If you're paying just a few dollars, the "jade" you get will be plastic or, at best, glass. But malas from Tibetan shops, yoga catalogs and websites that sell meditation supplies are as real as the ones worn by Buddhas in Tibet.



Phila McDaniel, a veteran American traveler who has collected prayer beads on each of her eight journeys to the Himalayan kingdom, recounts this story: "On a recent trip, my friend and I met three living buddhas. They gave each of us a bracelet mala. After my friend had gotten home to New York, she went into a coffee shop wearing hers. The waitress there was wearing an almost identical one. My friend asked the waitress if she had been to Tibet, too. 'Oh, no,' said the waitress. For heaven's sake, she'd gotten it in a department store!"

Tibetan members of the Khampa warrior group wear red or black silk twisted threads and circlets of mastadon ivory in their hair. This man is wearing coral prayer beads and dzi beads, a special banded agate with eye markings that symbolize the eyes of Buddha. Real dzi beads are so rare and expensive that a single one can cost a life savings.

# Prayer Beads in Other Religions

Holy Men of Katmandu, Nepal, equivalent to the living Buddhas in Tibet, are wanderers called Sudhus. They are highly revered for their knowledge, and people are eager to make donations to them. Their valuable and abundant ebony mala beads reflect their elevated position.

The Hindu/Buddhist mala is the Great Mother of rosaries. From India and the Himalayan kingdoms, it traveled east to China and Japan. It also traveled west to Africa and Europe, where it evolved into the Islamic subha, the Christian rosary, the Eastern Orthodox prayer rope, and the secular worry beads used throughout Greece and the Middle East.

Nearly two-thirds of the world's population prays or meditates with beads. Common to many strands is the number nine. Nine is the symbol of completion, for it is the highest of the single-digit numerals. Where the numbers don't add up to nine, often they are divisible by three, symbolic of the cosmic Trinities in Hinduism (Brahma, Vishnu, Shiva), Christianity (Father, Son, Holy Spirit), Goddess worship (maiden, mother, wise old woman), and the three central concepts of Buddhism (Buddha, Dharma, Sangha).

## The Islamic Subha

Called *subha*, from the Arabic to praise, the Muslim rosary has 99 beads, one for each name of Allah found in the Koran. It is believed that whoever recites these 99 names—as well as the phrase *Glory to Allah* on the long bead known as the imam or leader bead—will get into heaven. The subha is strung with markers after the 33rd and 66th beads. All kinds of stones are used in the making of these prayer beads, but the most beloved, says Lois Sherr Dubin in her book, *The History of Beads*, are from date pits that come from the sacred pilgrimage city of Mecca. Prayer beads are typically sold near places of worship, and Islamic subhas are no exception. You'll find vendors stationed outside mosques.

## The Roman Catholic Rosary

Within a circle of 54 beads—five sets of 10 small beads, each set separated by a distinctively larger bead—a devotee prays to the Blessed Virgin and to God the Father. A *Hail Mary* is recited at each small bead; a *Lord's Prayer* at the bigger interval bead. Devotees often make three tours around the rosary, meditating on specific New Testament events called the Mysteries. *Rosary* comes from the Latin *rosarium*, which means *rose garden*, probably a reference to the flower-filled cloister in a church or private residence where prayerful time could be passed in spiritual fullness and earthly beauty. The flower connection is interesting. *Mala*, remember, means *garland of flowers* in Sanskrit. What better object to suggest the evanescence of life is there but a flower? Here's another mystical connection: add five and four, and you get nine.

## Eastern Orthodox Prayer Ropes and Beads

In the Orthodox traditions of Turkey, Greece, Romania, and Russia, using prayer beads or knotted ropes is a monastic devotion, often (but not always) reserved for men. Depending on the particular tradition, a prayer strand may have 100 beads or 103. A Romanian Orthodox prayer rope made to be worn on the wrist has 33 knots. While most rosaries are strung in the traditional circular form, Russian Orthodox beads are strung in such a way as to resemble a ladder, a theme in keeping with the general Orthodox belief that prayer is the primary way for the soul to make its spiritual ascent to heaven. Central to Orthodoxy is a continual repetition of the Jesus Prayer: *Lord, Jesus Christ, Son of God, have mercy on me as a sinner*. The prayer is a means of achieving a spiritual union with God. The rope is used to count the number of times the prayer is said.

## Worry Beads

It is not unusual to see elderly men in Greece, Turkey, and elsewhere in the Middle East fingering secular beads, called *komboloi* (kom-bo-loy) in Greek. The 33-bead strand is not for prayer, but it does have a calming effect on those who hold it. Worry beads have become hip among young Greeks of both sexes, reports a recent story from Athens: "The komboloi is more than just a noisy trinket. It's a scrap of tradition amid an endless feast of foreign culture." There, as here, says the story, "It's suddenly cool to be with beads."

# Chakras:
## Your Portal to the Universe

*Chakra* is the Sanskrit word for *wheel of light*. You have seven such wheels—vortexes of energy—located at points along the spine. Like the soul, which you cannot see but perceive to be present, the chakras exist within you, spinning at the core of your being. Each chakra, in a color from red to violet, connects to a specific section of the human body. Meditating with a mala will help stimulate your chakras as you finger each bead. Beads made of certain materials will help open specific chakras. (See the Bead Chart in the next section.) Think of each chakra as a window that lets you see the world more clearly or, even better, a door that allows the awesome power of the universe to enter and flow within you.

## Power at Your Fingertips

Students of reflexology know that by massaging the sole of the foot, the whole body can be made to feel better. That's because both nerve endings and the more subtle meridians through which energy travels through the body have points of stimulation in the foot. That's true of hands as well. Fingering prayer beads of any sort—malas, rosaries, subhas, even worry beads—stimulates the higher chakras.

Each fingertip has a point that "awakens the senses," says Dr. Feng Liang, who practices Chinese acupuncture in New York City. This association is crosscultural. Yogis believe that the fingertips are linked to the Crown chakra, the energy vortex at the top of your head that connects you to existence beyond three dimensions (see Chakra chart, at right). In fact, the point of stimulation at the very tip of the finger pad corresponds exactly to the Crown chakra on your head.

Just stimulating this point is not enough, obviously, otherwise everyone tapping on a keyboard would be in the throes of cosmic ecstasy. But by focusing your attention through meditation or prayer, you channel your energy. Visualize how a swiftly running mountain river (you) empties into a vast, placid lake (your higher self).

Palmside below the fingertips, in the space between the first two finger creases, is the area that corresponds to the Third Eye chakra. The Third Eye is the seat of wisdom, insight, and harmony. Not coincidentally, this space is the place where the rosary rests as you are fingering the beads one at a time. No wonder you find a place of calmness in prayer. Body and mind are working in harmony to transport you there.

# Chakras

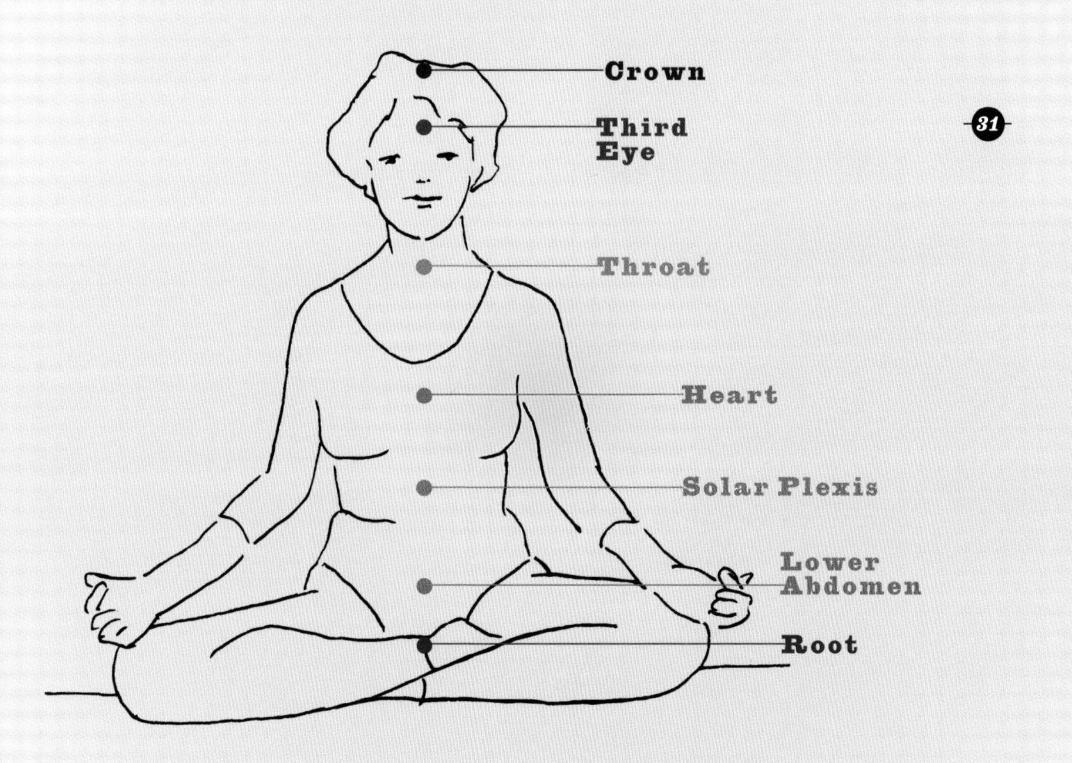

Crown
Third Eye
Throat
Heart
Solar Plexis
Lower Abdomen
Root

| | |
|---|---|
| **Root**<br>COLOR:<br>red<br>SYMBOL:<br>4-petal lotus | Situated at the very bottom of the spine, the Root chakra unites you to the physical world. It is the chakra of survival—the instinct to eat, to breathe, to make a place for yourself in the bosom of Mother Earth. Its energy is directed toward feet, legs, blood, large intestines. If you want to balance this chakra, get yourself a mala with brown, black, red, and iron-rich stones, like bloodstone or hematite, or a root wood like tulsi. |
| **Lower Abdomen**<br>COLOR:<br>orange<br>SYMBOL:<br>6-petal lotus | This is the chakra of reproductive and digestive organs and of the lower back and hips. The second chakra draws us to water and regulates our bodily fluids much as the moon governs the tides. Its energy is directed toward sexual passion, emotion, friendship. Is it any wonder that Aphrodite and Eros—Venus and Cupid—are the deities we associate with it? To balance and open this chakra, try a mala with orange stones such as coral or carnelian. |
| **Solar Plexis**<br>COLOR:<br>yellow<br>SYMBOL:<br>10-petal lotus | The solar plexus is the melting pot where physical and spiritual come together. This is where your "gut instinct"—the physical feeling—merges with the mental radar of intuitive perception. It is also where id instincts—overindulgence, for instance—are held in check by more reasoned thinking. To balance this chakra of balance, look for a mala with yellow stones such as amber, citrine, tiger's eye, or topaz. |

### Heart

COLOR:
green
SYMBOL:
12-petal
lotus

As the chakras rise up the spine, the impulses they inspire are of beauty, creativity, healing, compassion. This is the chakra that lets you "have a heart," be "warm-hearted" and "whole-hearted." Physically, it energizes not only the blood-pumping organ but the upper torso organs such as lungs. Whatever your religious leaning, there is a deity of beauty or compassion to guide you: Chinese Buddhist Kuan Yin, Tibetan Buddhist Tara, the Christian Virgin Mary, the Yoruba Oshun. To help you connect, look for a green-stone mala such as jade, or a heart-wood such as warm rosewood or fragrant sandalwood.



### Throat

COLOR:
turquoise
SYMBOL:
16-petal
lotus

Residing at the base of the neck between the collarbones, the fifth chakra is the vehicle of communication. This is the chakra that inspires you to express your feelings, to create, to sing, to speak out. It also helps you develop and listen to your *inner voice*—and to listen to the voices of others. A finely tuned fifth chakra also allows you to appreciate the more subtle sound of silence. Turquoise balances this chakra and draws its positive energy. Meditate with a turquoise-bead mala (or just wear one) to acquire a clear voice.

The lotus is a symbol for various chakras and, in Buddhism, a symbol for the true and untainted nature of beings.

## Third Eye

COLOR:
indigo
SYMBOL:
10-petal
lotus



The sixth chakra dwells behind the forehead. It is the seat of wisdom—knowledge beyond intelligence—that allows us to integrate our higher being with the everyday world. Philosophers called it "the seat of the soul." In physical terms this chakra is the pineal gland, which is activated by light coming through the eyes. It is associated with the brain, face, physical senses. To invite its energy, meditate with a mala that contains lapis lazuli or silver beads. You may want to invoke the spirit of Athena or Sarasvati, respectively Greek and Hindu goddesses of wisdom, or the elephant-trunked Ganesh, the Hindu god of spiritual insight.

## Crown

COLOR:
yellow
SYMBOL:
10-petal
lotus

The seventh chakra rests at the top of the head—just above the apex of the spinal cord, the brain—where it serves as a conduit between you and heaven. This chakra represents the totality of things: complete stillness, all knowledge, utter bliss, cosmic unity, the white light of all colors as they come together. Enlist the vibrational energy of a violet amethyst or clear crystal mala when you meditate, or one made of humble bodhi seeds, fruit of the tree under which an ordinary man became the Buddha.

Spheres
of Influence:
Beads
and What They
Do for You

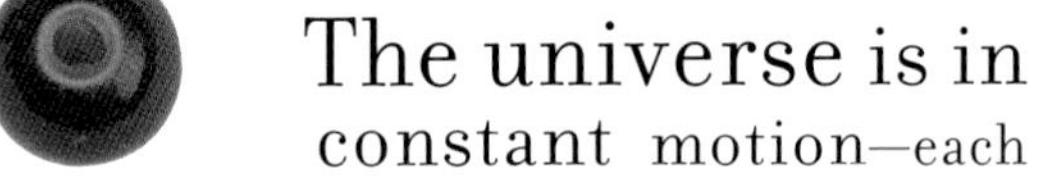

The universe is in constant motion—each element within it emitting its own particular electrical frequency or vibration—from the most distant celestial body to the most infinitesimal atom. Gemstones are particularly resonant. "Gemstones are crystals, and all crystals conduct energy," notes Guru Kirn. "We find crystals in radios, silicon chips, computers, watches—even submarines and rockets."

On a more subtle level, gemstones—along with wood, seeds, and other prayer-bead materials—work in harmony with the human aura, attracting the life-giving energy of the universe to you. They will enhance positive vibrations while drawing out or deflecting negative ones. With meditation or focused thought, that energy can be directed as precisely as a laser (which itself can use another gemstone: ruby).

How do you know what gemstone is the right one for you? Hold malas of various types in your hand, or finger the beads that will be strung into a mala. "Trust your intuition. You'll know which stones are right for you at a particular time," say Shakya Design's Kate and David Cowsky.



Don't be surprised if you find yourself drawn to carnelian, lapis lazuli, red coral, or turquoise. "These four gemstones will give every ounce of their being to heal you on all levels: physical, mental, and spiritual," says Guru Kirn. If you can't afford an entire strand of semiprecious beads, not to worry. Even a modest wooden-bead strand that contains a few special gemstones will resonate with their particular vibration.

Want to develop your intuition to better select the right beads for you? There are gemstones for that, too. The chart on the following pages brings together a patchwork of information about the materials from which prayer beads are made, the powers they hold, and how to direct them to your personal benefit. Whether you begin your search from Buddhist ideas, yoga, astrology, or crystal healing, you will find everything you need to connect with your own personal power mala.

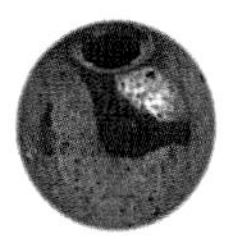

| **Mineral** | **Description** | **Spiritual Properties** |
|---|---|---|
| AGATE | A crystalline mineral found throughout the world, it is distinctive in its coloration—from pale yellow to clear blue to blood red to gray, brown, and black—and marked by kaleidoscopic patterns and graphic striations. Geodes are agate formations. | Agate calms the spirit and helps focus mental energy, so it is a good gemstone to meditate with or to use to center yourself when you are working on an important task. |
| AMBER | Smooth and honey-toned, this fossilized pine resin has been used since antiquity to make beads and amulets. In Tibet, where orthodox Buddhist teachings blend with indigenous folk practices, amber beads are believed to protect the wearer from evil spirits. Ancient Greeks believed amber fragments were the hardened rays of the sun. | Amber is a balancing stone that both calms and energizes the spirit. Yogis believe it awakens and stabilizes Kundalini (a powerful energy that rises through the chakras, awakening each in turn). |

| Physical Properties | Zodiac Signs | Planets, Element | Chakra |
|---|---|---|---|
| Releases stress and tension. Even if you are not using your mala to meditate, fingering the beads will help calm you. | Capricorn, Scorpio, Taurus | Mars, earth | Root |
| Energizes on a physical as well as spiritual plane. Eases aggression and tightness, promotes altruism and a more open personality. Soothes emotions during post-operative care. | Leo, Virgo, Sagittarius | Sun and Mars, fire | Solar Plexus |

Increasingly, people are wearing more than one kind of mala. The man here is wearing red beads, possibly carnelian and tiger's eye, among others.

| Mineral | Description | Spiritual Properties |
| --- | --- | --- |
| AMETHYST  | Perhaps because of its ethereal color—pale lavender to deep purple—this quartz gem has been used in many cultures to attract love. Its name is derived from the Greek *amethustos*—"not drunk"—so it has also been considered a protection against—and a help out of—intoxication and addiction. | Amethyst increases intuitive awareness, lifts the spirits, and protects against negative vibrations. Promotes a gentle spirit. Sleep with an amethyst stone or mala underneath your pillow and you may stimulate your creative mind. |
| AVENTURINE  | A light, almost translucent, green, this stone might be mistaken for pale jade, but it is in fact a type of quartzite. Aventurine fosters perception. In ancient Tibet it was used to improve eyesight; elsewhere today it is used to develop mental clarity. | Increases memory and mental acuity; fosters communication. Like other green stones, it helps open the Heart chakra to let you give and receive love. |

| Physical Properties | Zodiac Signs | Planets, Element | Chakra |
|---|---|---|---|
| If you want to stop smoking, to stay sober, to clean up your act, this is a good stone to help you. Aids in physical healing, reduces stress, brings serenity in times of grief. | Capricorn, Pisces | Jupiter and Neptune, water | Crown |
| Attracts prosperity, promotes fertility, engenders success. If you are starting a new business or setting off on a journey of any kind, wear a wrist mala made of this stone. | Leo, Libra | Mercury and Venus, air | Heart |

| Mineral | Description | Spiritual Properties |
| --- | --- | --- |
| BLOODSTONE | Along with carnelian, this stone—also called red jasper—is in the family of quartz gems known as chalcedony. Bloodstone is an ornamental favorite because it polishes brightly. Its deep red color connects it to iron in the earth and blood in the body. | A metaphysical transformer, bloodstone helps turn negative energy to positive energy, and emotional energy to spiritual energy. If you want to turn your life around, meditating with bloodstone beads may empower you. |
| CARNELIAN | This warm and beautiful gemstone was carved and strung as far back as the Neolithic Era, ten thousand years ago. Throughout history and cultures it has been considered a good-luck stone, attracting prosperity and repelling bad energy. | Promotes harmony, peace, optimism. Carnelian releases the negative emotions—anger, apathy, envy, fear, sorrow—while bolstering positive ones, such as patience and courage. |

| Physical Properties | Zodiac Signs | Planets, Element | Chakra |
|---|---|---|---|
| Regulates blood flow, hormone levels, heart health, cell structure. Helps heal the ovaries. | Capricorn, Scorpio, Taurus | Mars, earth | Root |
| As it is a healer of the spirit, so it is a healer of the body. Purifies the blood, increases passion, relieves PMS symptoms. If you're in a rut, this is the stone to get you moving. | Cancer, Libra, Scorpio | Sun and Mars, fire | Lower abdomen |

| Mineral | Description | Spiritual Properties |
|---|---|---|
| CITRINE | Citrine is a quartz gem. Its clear, sunny color encourages a bright outlook on life. Known as the "stone of abundance," it promotes spiritual and physical energy. In purely material terms, it seems to attract wealth and good fortune. | Use this gem to purify the aura, increase psychic awareness, or help raise self-esteem. Balances emotions—in fact, tipping them toward the positive. |
| CLEAR QUARTZ | Quartz is the most abundant mineral on earth (12 percent of the planet) and vibrates at the highest frequencies. In its transparency, crystal quartz suggests purity. It is thus a symbol of the human spirit in its most immaculate form. Its power evokes the great goddess; in Buddhist practice, Tara or Kuan Yin, the Bodhisattva of Compassion. | Clear quartz is a channeling stone. Its vibration purifies the spirit. In meditation, it will help you find a pathway to that which is beyond the five physical senses—your spirit, the angels, infinity. |

| Physical Properties | Zodiac Signs | Planets, Element | Chakra |
|---|---|---|---|
| Citrine detoxifies the body (it's another good stone to help you eliminate nicotine and other drugs), aids tissue regeneration, improves digestion. | Leo, Sagittarius, Virgo | Sun, fire | Solar plexus |
| Helps the body detoxify, relax, have a good heart in the physical as well as spiritual sense. Its energy will impart strength and vitality. Want to get your life organized? Meditate with a crystal mala. | Capricorn, Pisces | Sun and Moon, fire and water | Crown |

| Mineral | Description | Spiritual Properties |
|---|---|---|
| GARNET | Prized as a gem for over 5,000 years, the garnet gets its name from the Latin *granatus*, which means seedlike, because in its rock matrix it looks like seeds of the pomegranate. Since ancient times the garnet has been a stone of good health, good luck, and prosperity. | Promotes willpower and commitment by increasing the psychic energy you need to see things through; if you are ready to leave a bad relationship, begin exercising, or lose weight, meditating with a garnet mala will empower you. |
| HEMATITE | A shimmering silver-black, hematite is rich in iron, the main component of blood and the metal that responds to magnetic energy. It thus draws the Earth's awesome power to us, while pulling negative energy away from us. Ancient Greek and Roman warriors rubbed hematite powder over their bodies before battle. | Considered an "anti-stress stone," it reflects negative energy back to the sender. Buoys your ability to resist life's pressures. Enhances logic and mathematical thinking. Increases your personal magnetism. |

| Physical Properties | Zodiac Signs | Planets, Element | Chakra |
|---|---|---|---|
| Called the "sex stone," it revitalizes physical and sexual energy, heightens pleasure, increases fertility. More commercially minded? Guru Kirn calls it "a good stone for doing business." | Capricorn, Scorpio, Taurus | Mars, earth and fire | Root |
| Like other iron-rich stones, hematite's vibration positively affects kidney function, which purifies and strengthens the blood. Draws impurities out of the body. Use a hematite mala to help you feel grounded. | Capricorn, Scorpio, Taurus | Saturn, fire | Root |

| Mineral | Description | Spiritual Properties |
|---|---|---|
| JADE | Light to dark green (and sometimes yellow), this luminous stone has been cherished by the Chinese for more than 7,000 years; their poets called it "the concentrated essence of love." It is widely considered a good-luck stone. At the end of the nineteenth century two different minerals were discovered, which were both called jade: nephrite and jadeite. Both have similar properties. | Jade is a stone of healing and tranquility. It brings peace, clarity, understanding, wisdom to the spirit and the emotions. Helps open the heart for unconditional love. Represents the eternal. |
| LAPIS LAZULI | This noble stone has been mined for over 8,500 years. Its name comes from the Persian *lazhward*, which means *sky blue*. Ground into powder for paint, it was the original ultramarine blue. Throughout history it has been treasured by royalty, including the Egyptian pharaohs, as well as by people everywhere of more modest means. | Helps you focus your energy in prayer and meditation, which makes it an excellent stone for mala beads. Promotes intuition, fosters creativity, stimulates intellectual clarity. |

| Physical Properties | Zodiac Signs | Planets, Element | Chakra |
|---|---|---|---|
| Absorbs negative energy, letting you rebound swiftly after physical difficulty, such as minor surgery, or emotional ordeals such as job loss, divorce, arguments with loved ones. Heightens sense of touch. | Leo, Libra | Sun and Venus, air | Heart |
| Known as a stone of regeneration in many cultures—it is associated with the Buddha of Healing—it helps balance emotions, release tension, maintain courage. Strengthens bones, thyroid gland. | Aquarius, Pisces, Sagittarius | Mercury and Venus; air, earth, fire, water | Third Eye |

| Mineral | Description | Spiritual Properties |
| --- | --- | --- |
| MALACHITE | Its deep green, copper-rich color is evocative of all growing things. It is thus associated with personal and physical growth and with business expansion. On a higher level, it will encourage wisdom and patience. Malachite is regarded as a stone of healing. | Healing on a spiritual level means breaking down old patterns so that new ones can take root and grow. Meditating with a malachite mala may help you get beyond stress, negative thinking, or bad relationships. |
| MOONSTONE | Like its namesake, the moonstone is associated with all things tranquil and receptive: profound meditation, deepened intuition, calmness in a wakened state, and a restful, dream-filled sleep. | Moonstone deepens the *yin* or feminine energies in both sexes (these are energies that increase spiritual awareness, promote peace on all levels). Attracts spiritual and physical love. |

| Physical Properties | Zodiac Signs | Planets, Element | Chakra |
| --- | --- | --- | --- |
| "If you are attracted to this crystal, chances are you have a history of heart-related problems," says crystal healer Karen Ryan. Use a malachite mala to help attract positive energy to heart and kidneys. | Leo, Libra | Venus, air | Heart |
| As the moon controls the tides, moonstone acts on bodily fluids. In particular, it reduces water retention. A full moon is said to increase the powers of this gem, both physically and spiritually. | Cancer, Libra, Scorpio | Moon, water | Lower abdomen |

| Mineral | Description | Spiritual Properties |
| --- | --- | --- |
| ONYX | This dark stone, like all black, brown, and blood red gems, is related to the Root chakra. Root gems connect the user to the Earth at its most instinctual level—survival, procreation, energy, and ambition. | Onyx is a stone that grounds us, helping us attain stability, energy, self-control. Its higher vibration promotes inspirational calmness, direction, and mental focus. |
| PEARL | These creamy, almost translucent gems come from oysters and fresh-water mussels, where they grow naturally or are cultivated. Round, irregular, or seedlike, all pearls are primarily calcium carbonate, as is mother-of-pearl, which lines the inner shell of many mollusks. Yogi Bhajan meditates with a pearl mala. | Pearls draw to you the great energy of the ocean. They inspire honesty, regeneration, and psychic and creative powers. They help balance the emotions, attract love. |

| Physical Properties | Zodiac Signs | Planets, Element | Chakra |
|---|---|---|---|
| This "stone of hard work" inspires us to direct our efforts and ambition to a safe home, a good job, food on the table. | Capricorn, Scorpio, Taurus | Mars and Saturn, fire | Root |
| Pearls not used as gemstones are ground up and used in vitamins as a source of calcium, thus they promote bone growth. Metaphysically, they help the body do the same. Pearls have a vibration that attracts wealth. | Cancer, Libra, Scorpio | Moon, water | Lower abdomen |

| Mineral | Description | Spiritual Properties |
| --- | --- | --- |
| RED CORAL | Coral has traveled from its place of harvest in warm Mediterranean and South Pacific oceans to such diverse locales as the mountains of Tibet, where it occupies a special place in mala rosaries, and the American Southwest, where it is revered by Native Americans as "the blood of Mother Earth." | Menstrual red in color, it encourages both sexes to develop their female side. Helps new mothers bond with their babies and all adults to make peace with their inner child. Meditating with red coral will summon inner strength. |
| ROSE QUARTZ | Like clear quartz, this translucent crystal with the lovely rose hue has a finely tuned vibration for channeling and healing. Aligned with the Heart chakra, it is especially adept at mending matters of romance and relationships. For this reason it is often called "the love stone." | Its vibration helps you channel negative energy away from you, filling the void with kindness and compassion. You are thus better equipped to give and receive love—romantic, familial, and platonic. Heightens awareness and appreciation of beauty in nature and art. |

| Physical Properties | Zodiac Signs | Planets, Element | Chakra |
|---|---|---|---|
| Strengthens women's reproductive organs. In both sexes, purifies kidneys, promotes blood circulation. Encourages passion. | Cancer, Libra, Scorpio | Moon and Venus, water | Lower abdomen |
| Physically, rose quartz helps you attain good health—to be, as its delicate color suggests, "in the pink." Meditate with a mala containing at least some of these stones, and you will notice a marked decrease in stress. | Leo, Libra | Venus, air | Heart |

A different kind of traditional prayer beads with silver and bone on the end.

| Mineral | Description | Spiritual Properties |
| --- | --- | --- |
| SILVER | For over six thousand years this soft, lustrous, extremely ductile metal has been mined and wrought for jewelry, ornaments, and monetary coins. Silver is the best-known reflector of visible light, which is why it has been used as a mirror backing. It is an excellent conductor of heat and electricity. | Metaphysically, it reflects negative energy back onto the sender, so you are protected from the bad vibes of those who would wish you ill. Conducts excess energy, thus helping to balance the aura. Helps develop the intuition. |
| SMOKY QUARTZ  | The hazy gray or brown—sometimes black—color of this quartz gemstone would suggest that it has something to hide, but nothing could be further from the truth. Smoky quartz does much to bring negative emotions out into the open where they can dissipate. This stone creates an energy field that protects you. | An emotional balancer, it modifies mood swings that result from life's big and little difficulties, PMS, and the hormonal ups and downs of menopause. Meditate with a smoky quartz mala to help lift stress or depression. |

| Physical Properties | Zodiac Signs | Planets, Element | Chakra |
|---|---|---|---|
| Eases stress, improves your ability to communicate. Materially, this money metal attracts wealth, as "it takes money to make money." Even silver plating may afford you some of this metal's power. | Cancer | Moon and Mercury, water and air | Third Eye |
| Its vibration is an aid to physical healing. If you turn to tobacco to deal with stress, try taking a "smoky quartz break" instead. Meditating with a mala that includes these gems may be similarly helpful to fight the urge to overindulge in food or drink. | Capricorn, Scorpio, Taurus | Mars, earth | Root |

| Mineral | Description | Spiritual Properties |
| --- | --- | --- |
| TIGER'S EYE | This brown quartz gem dances with an almost otherworldly yellow-gold glow (courtesy of iron oxides). Cut and polished, it does indeed resemble a feline eye. It combines the groundedness of Earth with the fire of higher passion. The Dalai Lama is known to use a tiger's eye mala. | Meditating with a tiger's eye mala is like taking a metaphysical vitamin—it increases courage and confidence, the inner resources necessary to set and achieve life goals. Promotes clear judgment. |
| TOPAZ | Topaz is considered a good-luck stone, drawing toward it good energy and courage for those who wear it or meditate with beads made from it. Its sunny yellow coloring promotes a similar disposition. | Like other yellow gems connected with the Solar Plexus chakra, it acts to release aggression and promote peace. Want to relax enough to "go with the flow"? Topaz is your gem. |

| Physical Properties | Zodiac Signs | Planets, Element | Chakra |
|---|---|---|---|
| Like all quartz crystals, tiger's eye has a finely tuned vibration. It increases energy flow, promotes wealth and prosperity. | Leo, Sagittarius, Virgo | Sun and Mars, fire | Lower abdomen |
| Helps detoxify liver, spleen, and other digestive organs. Meditate with a topaz mala to find a balance between the material and the spiritual. | Leo, Sagittarius, Virgo | Sun and Mars, fire | Solar Plexus |



The Dalai Lama is known to use a tiger's eye mala.

Women often weave lengths of beads into their hair, and sometimes they fashion it with 108 braids—a sacred number. Sometimes women will sell or trade beads they are wearing.

| Mineral | Description | Spiritual Properties |
|---|---|---|
| TOURMALINE  | Here is a quartz crystal with many chromatic personalities. It may be red, pink, yellow, green, blue, violet, or even clear. Crystals with two or more colors are striking but not uncommon. | A stone or bead that brings together complementary colors, such as red and green, suggests balance—a coming together of opposites. Adding a few of these stones to your mala may help keep you on an even keel. |
| TURQUOISE  | Turquoise—the name of the stone is descriptive of its color—was first mined in the Middle East over 6,000 years ago. It got its lovely name courtesy of geography. Its trade passage to Europe was through Turkey, and *turquoise* is French for *Turkish*. It is considered a stone of healing, of good luck, and of friendship. | Its vibration absorbs impurities on all levels. Generally regarded as protective. If you feel the call to be a healer, turquoise may help you develop these abilities. Meditate with a turquoise mala if you are seeking improved health for yourself, a friend, or a loved one. |

| Physical Properties | Zodiac Signs | Planets, Element | Chakra |
|---|---|---|---|
| Tourmaline relieves fatigue and anemia. Helps balance the energy of your lower abdominal organs, such as kidney and bladder. | Cancer, Libra, Scorpio | Venus and Mars, water | Lower abdomen |
| Connected to the Throat chakra, it will help you develop a strong, clear voice—whether to sing, to chant, to lecture, or to speak out for good causes and against unjust ones. | Aquarius, Gemini, Taurus | Mercury and Venus, air | Throat |

| Wood, Seed, or Bone | Description | Properties |
|---|---|---|
| BODHI SEED | It was while meditating under a bodhi tree that Prince Siddhartha attained enlightenment and became the Buddha. The dark-speckled seeds from this fig tree thus have special meaning for all seekers of divine wisdom. *Bodhi* in Sanskrit is *enlightenment*. | Eternal wisdom is not guaranteed, of course, but meditating—or just sitting quietly—with a bodhi-seed mala offers an opportunity for serenity because it connects you mentally, perhaps spiritually, to the Buddha. You just have to take a few minutes out of your busy day. |
| BONE | In subsistence cultures where nothing is wasted, animal bone—from yak, camel, or other beasts of burden—is used for ornamentation, both secular and ritualistic. Bone beads, often strung with a few precious pieces of coral or amber, are a traditional material for malas in the Himalayas. At the monasteries, one might encounter a devout practitioner with a mala made from bones of a holy monk or revered lama. | Bone beads remind us that life is fleeting. For the same reason, some malas contain tiny skulls carved from animal bone. Macabre? No more so than the Mexican *Dia de los Muertes* (Day of the Dead), a celebration of beloved ancestors, or our Halloween, which precedes the Christian All Souls' Day. |

| Wood, Seed, or Bone | Description | Properties |
|---|---|---|
| EBONY | This dark, heavy wood comes from the heart of a tree that grows in India, South Asia, and Africa. The dark core is found under layers of almost pure white wood, a suggestion that things are not always what they seem—and a metaphor that operates on both physical and spiritual levels. | Ebony has been used traditionally for ceremonial objects, not only mala rosaries but Indian scepters and African sculptures. The more you handle it, the more beautiful it becomes, which makes it an ideal bead for meditation. |
| LOTUS | The sacred Indian lotus symbolizes purity and birth. As the fabled thousand-petaled blossom, it is the symbol of compassionate Kuan Yin, because it represents rebirth on a higher plane—enlightenment. In more physical terms, it is a water lily whose slightly oval, matte brown seeds, which are about the size of your pinky fingertip, have been strung into rosaries since ancient times. | Lotus seeds are connected not only to Kuan Yin, but to Lakshmi, a generous Hindu goddess who is prayed to for the prosperity and good fortune she bestows. You might cover all bases with a mala that includes lotus seeds as well as a few gems that attract luck or wealth, such as aventurine, citrine, garnet, or pearl. |

| Wood, Seed, or Bone | Description | Properties |
|---|---|---|
| ROSEWOOD | With their deep roots and outstretched limbs, trees represent the human longing to reach to the heavens—to connect with the eternal—while remaining grounded, steadfast, and true. The rosewood tree does this with a warm heart—a core that is deep red to rich purplish brown. | Use this beautiful wood to cultivate the qualities associated with an ardent heart: compassion, kindness, and love. Rosewood has been used traditionally to fashion xylophone keys, so don't overlook its strong vibrational quality, physical and otherwise. |
| RUDRAKSHA | Dark red with a grooved, deeply convoluted surface, the small rudraksha nut was first strung into a mala more than one thousand years ago. It is revered by followers of the Hindu god Shiva, the divine destroyer. This sacred seed is sold for pennies a handful in temple stalls throughout India, allowing even the poorest devotee to afford a rosary. | The rough surface of the rudraksha seed represents the ascetic life required for the worship of Shiva. Whatever your beliefs, its texture encourages us to contemplate (and accept) the fact that things do not always go smoothly. |

| Wood, Seed, or Bone | Description | Properties |
|---|---|---|
| SANDALWOOD | Sandalwood trees have been cultivated since antiquity for their ceremonial and ritual use. This is the wood used in King Solomon's temple. In powdered form, sandalwood creates the paste that is applied to make Brahmin caste marks. It is considered an auspicious wood. | Beads made from this fragrant heartwood bring a sensory element to meditation, reminding us that sitting in thought or prayer need not be austere but can be deeply pleasurable. You may find that simply inhaling the aroma of your sandalwood beads can help you return to that quietness. |
| TULSI | The pesto sauce you put on your pasta comes from a basil plant closely related to India's sacred tulsi bush. Followers of Vishnu, the Hindu god revered for his goodness and mercy, use tulsi malas, the beads of which are made from the upper root and stem of the dried plant. | You don't have to be Hindu to connect with this plant, just someone who appreciates the glorious web of cross-cultural connections. The Greeks, for instance, bring sprigs of basil to church to be blessed—on St. Basil's Day—which they use to purify their homes and to ensure health for the year. |

# Making Your Own Malas

Of the many bead materials traditionally strung into malas, the three you have are among the most venerable: earthy red carnelian, which carries with it good luck and healing energies; glistening tiger's eye, which inspires courage and confidence; and warm sandalwood, which evokes both the rootedness of a tree and the quiet calm of a forest. The process for making each one is the same, as we show and explain in this chapter.

If you're making a mala to help you connect with the spiritual traditions of Buddhism or Hinduism, you may want to approach mala making as a meditation, focusing on the process as a means of centering yourself.

Making your own malas can be an occasion for a gathering of friends, as well as something one does by one's self.

Following are some things you can do to enhance the process:

- Sound a small gong to signal for yourself the beginning of the mala-making meditation.

- Burn incense to permeate the space in which you are working. Its scent will remind you of the special nature of your project.

- Have a lighted candle on your worktable. Should your mind wander while you're working, focus on the flame to help you focus on the project.

- Play meditative music. Anything that calms the body and stills the spirit is a good choice, whether that's Mozart, shakuhachi flute, European choral music, Native American drumming, or Tibetan chants. In keeping with the Buddhist nature of the beads, we've listed a few CDs of Tibetan Buddhist chants and related music (see page 77).

Any corner of your room can become a sacred space with perhaps a candle, some incense, a statue of the Buddha.

If you take a more Western approach to the mala—that is, you're thinking of it as jewelry—then you'll find a convivial group "string-along" a lot of fun.

When you're finished, sharing your bracelets with others is a wonderful way to exercise a little karma yoga, the doing of good deeds. However, there's no reason you can't give in to the urge to wear your three bracelets at once, for their various properties create a tapestry of psychic dynamism that can inspire and energize you—kind of a breakfast, lunch, and dinner of metaphysical nutrition.

## The materials

Your kit has 27 beads each of carnelian, tiger's eye, and sandalwood, two wooden separator beads for each mala, and a two-part head bead for each mala.



You'll string your beads on a red cord. Red symbolizes the bloodline of the Buddha flowing through the centuries. Other materials to have on hand: fine wire or paper clip to help you string the head bead, and a wire cutter.

In this box are three sets of beads, enough to make three different 27-bead malas: carnelian, tiger's eye, and sandalwood.

## Step One: Stringing the head bead

You'll start with the large, three-holed bead, variously called head bead, guru bead, or mother bead [shown at right]. This is actually a two-part bead. In Step Four, you'll add the smaller cup-like part.

To begin: Cut an eight-inch length of fine wire and loop it in half. Holding the head bead so that holes are at "three o'clock", "six o'clock", and "nine o'clock", insert the looped wire in at "six" and out at "three." Thread the cord through the wire loop, pulling the cord completely through the bead. To keep the head bead from slipping off the cord, sandwich the "six o'clock" end between two layers of tape, which you'll remove when you're finished.

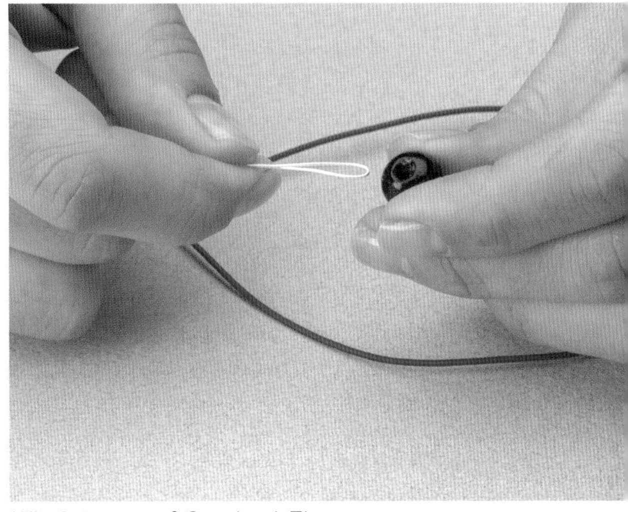

What's in a name? Guru bead: The guru symbolizes the teachers in our lives. (*Gu* in Sanskrit means darkness, and *ru* means light.) A guru, or teacher, takes you from the darkness of ignorance to the light of wisdom. Mother bead: The mother symbolizes creation, existence, and the all-pervasive spirit of things.

## Questions and Answers

**Q:** *Can I combine different stones on one mala?*

Yes, indeed. There's a tradition of combining beads on one mala. When you're selecting beads, you may choose specific stones for their specific vibrations or simply allow yourself to be drawn intuitively to the stones whose power you need most. Arrange them in a pattern that's pleasing to you. At Sacred Gems, Guru Kirn has a lovely 54-bead mala made from the four healing stones: the blues of turquoise and lapis alternating with the orange-reds of carnelian and coral.

## Step Two: Stringing the first six beads

Now thread six beads, one by one, onto the "three o'clock" end of the cord. We're stringing carnelian, but the process is the same for sandalwood and tiger's eye. The hole in all these beads is large enough for the cord to pass through without the wire threader. If you like, you can stiffen the very end of the cord by rubbing it over the surface of a candle.

(As you look at malas from different cultures, you'll note that some have individual knots between the beads. This is especially true of beads with monetary or trading value, such as amber, jade, or lapis. Individual knotting is not necessary, and we do not do it here.)

## Step Three: Adding the separator bead

After six carnelian beads, thread one separator bead onto the cord. Add 15 more carnelian beads, then add another separator bead. Finish with six more carnelian beads. The rhythm is six, spacer, 15, spacer, six. If you're keeping track of the beads, you'll realize that the separators are not part of the count of 27. Separators—which could be any color or material—provide a place for you to pause reflectively. Think of them as quiet islands in the serene lake of meditation or prayer.

Shakya Designs' Kate and David Cowsky use wooden beads mixed with a sprinkling of semi-precious stones, depending on their customer's wishes or their sense of what's right for the person. At Shasta Abbey, for instance, they offer a sandalwood wrist rosary with carnelian divider beads and one in rosewood with lapis lazuli.

**Q:** *How about combining my malas with other jewelry?*

Malas are so distinctive that other jewelry is really not necessary, particularly if you wear several malas at once. But, hey, you're not living a monastic existence, so go ahead and mix your malas with other things if you want. Even devout Buddhists who are out in the world are known to strap on a watch now and then.

**Q:** *Can I add something personal to my mala? (I was thinking about a small locket with a picture of my departed and much beloved aunt.)*

If adding a personal item allows you to have a deeper, more meditative experience, why not? A personal object—a locket or an item owned by a loved one—creates a kind of spiritual charm bracelet. It's a tangible reminder that although you are on different planes of

## Step Four: Back to the head bead

As you come around to the head bead—both in the making of your mala and in your meditation with it—you are reminded of the cyclical nature of things, that the end is also the beginning. Thread the bead using the wire hook, as you did in Step One. Here, though, your loop will exit at "nine o'clock." Insert the red cord and pull it through, so that both ends are now emerging from the bottom of the head bead. The enclosure you have just created is a sacred space. Now take both ends of the cord and draw them through the cuplike bead that completes the head bead. The hole in this bead is large enough to accommodate both cords.

## Step Five: Finishing your mala

The simplest way to finish your mala is to tie the ends with an ordinary square knot, pictured. Leave two inches of cord visible, as this is your reminder of the Buddha.

## Step Six: A Mala meditation

If you feel yourself drawn into the circle of energy created by your completed mala, you may want to make a small meditation. Assume a comfortable sitting position—cross-legged on the floor, or sitting straight in a chair with your feet on the ground—and reflect on the ideas contained within your mala: the Buddha who flows from generation to generation; the endless cycle of birth and death; the power of the teachers in our lives.

existence, you are not really apart. Some of Shasta Abbey's malas feature a delicate jade Kuan Yin suspended from the guru bead. In a related way, you might want to add to your mala a small crucifix, mezuzah, or other object evocative of the religion you grew up with. All too often we shed one set of beliefs for another, but past and present are just different points on the timeline of life. "In Tibet, where religion is not detached from life," says author Lois Sherr Dubin, "it is even common to find personal odds and ends, such as tweezers or keys, attached to the rosaries."

There's no limit to the kinds of things you can reflect on, so dwell on whatever moves you, whatever you feel comfortable with. An alternative, especially if you've been making malas with friends, is to wind down your activities with a "tea ceremony" of your own devising.

## Safekeeping

Your wrist mala is more than just jewelry. When you're not wearing or using it, slip it into a pouch, envelope, or box for safekeeping. The containers here were made especially for malas, but you can convert any small object, such as a belt pack or cloth purse, into a mala holder.

## Meditation Music

Music can create and maintain a contemplative mood. Here we focus on the mantras, rhythms, and harmonies of the various Buddhist traditions. We found these titles from www.fourgates.com.

**CHANT OF REPENTANCE:** A mantra to help you clear past karma. Play it while making a mala or meditating with it. **DHAMA SUNA:** Music for wisdom and enjoyment—19 Tibetan Buddhist devotional pieces performed by a chorus of lamas and musicians. **HOMAGE OF AMITABHA BUDDHA, CHINESE BUDDHIST RESEARCH INSTITUTE:** This is a chant to the Buddha who oversees the heavenly realm of Amitabha. **MORNING AND EVENING CHANTING, CHINESE BUDDHIST RESEARCH INSTITUTE:** Traditional chants to open and close the day. **OM TARA, A BUDDHIST MANTRA FOR MEDITATION:** Tara is the Bodhisattva of Compassion in the Tibetan Buddhist tradition. **OM MANI PADME HUM: THE MANTRA OF AVALOKITESHVARA:** This six-syllable mantra, translated as "Hail, Jewel in the Lotus," is directed to Kuan Yin, the Bodhisattva of Compassion in the Chinese Buddhist tradition. **PRAISE OF SAKYAMUNI LORD BUDDHA:** A chant in honor of the Great Teacher. **SOUND OF THE COSMOS, FAN LI-BIN:** Serene and blissful harmonies. **TIBET: MONKS OF SERA JE MONASTERY:** Ritual Music and Chants of the Gelug Tradition. **TRADITIONAL TIBETAN CHANTS:** Tibetan Buddhist Songs and Chants, Choying Drolma and the Nuns of Nagi Gompa Monastery. **CHANTS OF DEVOTION.**

And these come from the Inner Dimension Catalog:

**CHAKRA CHANTS, JONATHAN GOLDMAN:** Each selection, in Tibetan overtone chanting, focuses on one of the seven chakras; **RHYTHMS OF THE CHAKRAS, GLEN VELEZ:** This master drummer has created rhythms, overtones, and harmonies to energize each of the body's seven energy sites.

# Photo Credits

ii– PhotoDisc

v– Jeffrey Aaronson/Network Aspen

vi (chpt opener)–*A monk in Lhasa, Tibet entwines his 108-bead mala around his hands expressing both his comfort with them and devotion to them as a significant part of his life. This is a common sight in Lhasa, where most of the people have come on their pilgrimage to the Jokang Temple.*

vii– Kurt Thorson

2– top: Brooks Kraft/Corbis Sygma

bottom: Glen Allison/PhotoDisc

3 (chpt opener)– Craig Lovell

*Ancient scriptures are stored inside the newly restored Tashi Gomang Assembly Hall at Drigung Monastery in Tibet.*

4– Robert & Linda Mitchell

7– right: Phila McDaniel

10– Jeffrey Aaronson/Network Aspen

13– Robert & Linda Mitchell

14– Index Stock Imagery

17 (chpt opener)–Galen Rowell *A gilded wall painting in the ruins of Ronbuk Monastery beneath Chomolugma (Mt. Everest) at 29, 108 feet.*

19– Craig Lovell

20– Elissa D'Elia

21– Craig Lovell

22– Phila McDaniel

24– Phila McDaniel

27– Audrey Gottlieb

29– Tim Brown/Tony Stone Images

30– Jeffrey Aaronson/Network Aspen

33– CMCD/PhotoDisc

35 (chpt opener)–Phila McDaniel

*A Buddha in Chengde, China.*

38–Arpad Benedek/iStockphoto.com (agate); Karol Kozlowski/iStockphoto.com (amber)

39– Elissa D'Elia

40–Edward Karaa/iStockphoto.com (amethyst); Arpad Benedek/iStockphoto.com (aventurine)

42–Arpad Benedek/iStockphoto.com (carnelian)

44–Edward Karaa/iStockphoto.com (citrine); Terry Wilson/iStockphoto.com (clear quartz)

48–Arpad Benedek/iStockphoto.com (lapis lazuli)